TAKE A BATH!

HEALTHY BODY HABITS

Mary Elizabeth Salzmann

Consulting Editor,
Diane Craig, M.A./ Reading Specialist

Sandcastle

An Imprint of Abdo Publishing
www.abdopublishing.com

www.abdopublishing.com

Published by Abdo Publishing, a division of ABDO, PO Box 398166, Minneapolis, Minnesota 55439. Copyright © 2015 by Abdo Consulting Group, Inc. International copyrights reserved in all countries. No part of this book may be reproduced in any form without written permission from the publisher. SandCastle™ is a trademark and logo of Abdo Publishing.

Printed in the United States of America, North Mankato, Minnesota
102014
012015

THIS BOOK CONTAINS RECYCLED MATERIALS

Editor: Alex Kuskowski
Content Developer: Nancy Tuminelly
Cover and Interior Design: Colleen Dolphin, Mighty Media, Inc.
Photo Credits: Shutterstock

Library of Congress Cataloging-in-Publication Data

Salzmann, Mary Elizabeth, 1968- author.

  Take a bath! : healthy body habits / Mary Elizabeth Salzmann.

     pages cm. -- (Healthy habits)

  Audience: Ages 4-9.

  ISBN 978-1-62403-532-6 (alk. paper)

  1. Baths--Health aspects--Juvenile literature. 2. Hygiene--Juvenile literature. 3. Health--Juvenile literature. [1. Cleanliness.] I. Title. II. Series: Salzmann, Mary Elizabeth, 1968- Healthy habits.

  RA780.S25 2015

  613.41--dc23

                    2014023598

SandCastle™ Level: Transitional

SandCastle™ books are created by a team of professional educators, reading specialists, and content developers around five essential components—phonemic awareness, phonics, vocabulary, text comprehension, and fluency—to assist young readers as they develop reading skills and strategies and increase their general knowledge. All books are written, reviewed, and leveled for guided reading, early reading intervention, and Accelerated Reader® programs for use in shared, guided, and independent reading and writing activities to support a balanced approach to literacy instruction. The SandCastle™ series has four levels that correspond to early literacy development. The levels are provided to help teachers and parents select appropriate books for young readers.

EMERGING · BEGINNING · **TRANSITIONAL** · FLUENT

CONTENTS

WHAT IS A HEALTHY HABIT?

Keeping your body clean is a healthy **habit**.

Cleaning your body gets rid of **germs**. Germs can make you and other people sick.

You feel good
when your body
is fresh and clean.

You keep your body clean by taking a bath or **shower** every day.

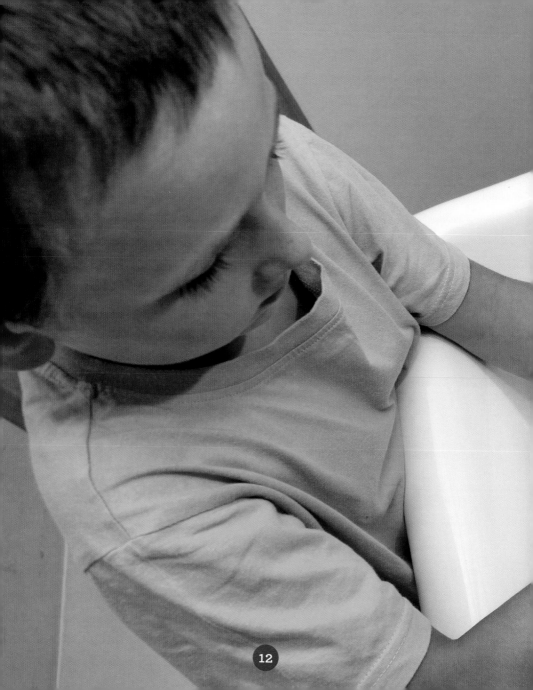

Wash your hands often. Then you won't spread **germs**.

Wear clean clothes and keep your hair neat. That is also part of having a clean body.

Owen takes a bubble bath. He wears a swim mask in the bath.

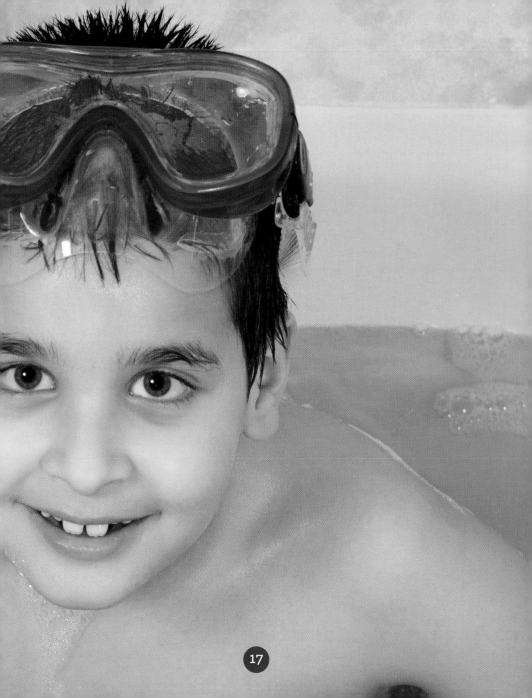

Julia combs her hair.
She gets all of the
tangles out.

David helps do the **laundry**. Then he will have clean clothes to wear.

How do you keep
your body clean?

HEALTH QUIZ

1. You don't feel good when your body is fresh and clean. True or False?

2. You should keep your body clean by taking a bath or **shower** once a month. True or False?

3. Washing your hands keeps you from spreading **germs**.
   True or False?

4. Owen wears a swimsuit in the bath. True or False?

5. Julia gets all of the tangles out of her hair. True or False?

Answers: 1. False 2. False 3. True 4. False 5. True

GLOSSARY

germ – a tiny, living organism that can make people sick.

habit – a behavior done so often that it becomes automatic.

laundry – clothes that have been or are being washed.

shower – a bath taken under a spray of falling water.

tangle – hair that is twisted or knotted together.